THE WATER PATROL

Saving Surfers' Lives in Big Waves

by Linda Barr

Reading Consultant:
Timothy Rasinski, Ph.D.
Professor of Reading Education
Kent State University

Content Consultant:
Eric Akiskalian
Extreme surfer and President of the
Association of Professional Towsurfers

Red Brick™ Learning

Published by Red Brick™ Learning
7825 Telegraph Road, Bloomington, Minnesota 55438
http://www.redbricklearning.com

Library of Congress Cataloging-in-Publication Data
Barr, Linda, 1944–
    The water patrol: saving surfers' lives in big waves / by Linda Barr;
reading consultant, Timothy Rasinski.
        p. cm.—(High five reading)
    Includes bibliographical references and index.
    ISBN 0-7368-5749-4 (soft cover)—ISBN 0-7368-5739-7 (hard cover)
    1. Lifeguards—Juvenile literature. I. Rasinski, Timothy V. II. Title.
III. Series.
GV838.72.B37 2006
797.2'1'0289—dc22
                            2005011160

Created by Kent Publishing Services, Inc.
Designed by Signature Design Group, Inc.
Edited by Jerry Ruff, Managing Editor, Red Brick™ Learning
Red Brick™ Learning Editorial Director: Mary Lindeen

This publisher has made every effort to trace ownership of all copyrighted
material and to secure necessary permissions. In the event of any questions
arising as to the use of any material, the publisher, while expressing regret for
any inadvertent error, will be happy to make necessary corrections.

Photo Credits:
Cover, pages 7, 11, 12, 17, 19, 20, 25, 26, 29, 31, 32, 35, Eric Akiskalian,
Towsurfer.com; page 4, Ron Brazil, Zuma Press; page 9, Ryan Casey; pages 15,
36, Tony Canadas; page 23, Terry Schmitt, UPI Photo Service; page 37, Erik
Aeder; page 39, Ron Dahlquist; page 41, Kevin Sullivan, KRT Photos; page 43,
Darin Fentiman, Zuma Press

Printed in the United States of America.

1 2 3 4 5 6 11 10 09 08 07 06 05

Table of Contents

Hawaiian Islands

Kauai

Oahu

Molokai

Maui

Hawaii

CHAPTER 1

Monster Waves

"That's the one, Pete!" Josh shouts.

*Josh points to a large **swell** far out in the ocean.*

Josh and Pete are surfing in Hawaii (hah-WYE-ee).

Hawaii has some of the biggest waves in the world.

Getting to the Big Waves

Surfers love to ride the big waves in Hawaii.
Some waves can rise to 80 feet (24 meters).
That's as high as an eight-story building!

These really big waves are far from shore.
Surfers need to be **towed** to get to them.
Pete is using a personal watercraft (PWC)
to tow Josh.

---

swell (SWEL): the top of a wave that has not fallen over
tow (TOH): to pull something behind you

Catching the Wave

As Pete and Josh get close to the swell, another big wave smashes into them. Luckily, they do not get pushed under the water.

Pete is able to tow Josh into the swell. The best place to start surfing is just below the top of a swell.

Josh stands on his **towboard**. He bends his knees and lets go of the **towrope**. Pete speeds away. He will pick Josh up after Josh rides the big wave.

Balancing on his board, Josh slides down the front of the monster wave. He is falling so fast he feels like he is floating. Even so, Josh can't stay ahead of the crashing swell.

---

towboard (TOH-bord): a surfboard that has bindings on it to connect a surfer's feet to the board
towrope (TOH-rohp): a rope tied to a boat that pulls a surfer

This surfer just caught a monster 68-foot (21-meter) wave.

Wipeout!

The wave has been breaking just behind Josh. Soon the **curl** catches him. It pounds him 30 feet (9 meters) under the water!

Josh tries not to **panic**. He gets his head above water once, but the next wave pushes him under again. Pete can't get close enough to pick Josh up. The water is too rough. Josh is tumbling like a beach toy under the water.

Then, two strong hands grab Josh. They pull him from the water. The water patrol has saved him!

What is the water patrol? Who would risk their lives to save surfers out riding the monster waves? How do these waves get so big, anyway?

---

curl (KURL): the top of the wave as it bends over
panic (PAN-ik): to be affected by sudden, great fear

A surfer on a PWC comes to help another surfer.

A Closer Look at Waves

The size and power of waves depend on wind and the shape of the ocean floor.

As wind blows across the ocean, it makes the water pile up. Waves form. Storms have strong winds, so they cause big waves. The waves that reach Hawaii may be caused by storms that happen as far away as Japan.

*Waves in Hawaii
can be very big.*

Even Higher

As waves get near land, they start to rub against the ocean floor. This makes the waves grow even higher. The more the floor **slopes**, the higher the waves grow. Near Hawaii, the waves can be very big and dangerous!

---

slope (SLOHP): to slant or tilt

*Laird Hamilton, the king of towsurfing,
catches a big wave.*

CHAPTER 2

The Hawaiian Water Patrol

Years ago, surfers rode only waves close to shore.
They could not get to the really big waves farther out.
These big waves were too far and moved too fast.
No one could paddle a surfboard out and catch them.
Surfers could only dream about riding these big waves.

A Change in Surfing

In the early 1990s, Laird Hamilton and his friends were using a boat to pull each other on surfboards. This gave them an idea.

This group of surfers began to use a PWC to tow each other out to the really big waves. Tow-in surfing or "towsurfing" was born!

Big waves can also be big trouble, however. Big-wave wipeouts can be deadly!

Close Call

More and more people started towsurfing.
Surfers also started to compete in big-wave
surfing contests.

Brian Keaulana (kee-oh-LAHN-uh) was
surfing in a big-wave contest in 1987.
He wiped out on a 20-foot (6-meter) wave.
Brian lost his board. Wave after wave crashed
down on him. Brian could barely take a
breath before the next wave hit. He felt like
he might drown.

*Mike Brummit falls in front of a
big swell near the northern California coast.*

The Plan

A friend rode up to Brian on a PWC.
The friend could not rescue him, though.
There was no room for Brian on the PWC.
The friend had to **flee** the pounding waves.

Finally, Brian made it to shore. He then
decided he had to find a way to use PWCs
to rescue surfers.

Brian asked his friend Terry Ahue
(AH-who-ee) to help. The two men formed
a team of surfers and **lifeguards**.

This team invented a rescue sled. The sled
hooks to the back of a PWC. To rescue a
surfer, one person drives the PWC.
Another rides on the sled. The one on the
sled pulls the struggling surfer onto the sled.
The PWC then tows the sled to safety.

---

flee (FLEE): to run away
lifeguard (LIFE-gard): a person trained to save
swimmers in danger

Two men show how to make a proper rescue with a PWC.

Big-Wave Surfing

Brian and Terry formed the Hawaiian Water Patrol. Soon the team was asked to help at big-wave surfing contests.

Big-wave surfing contests take place far from shore. There, the waves can be 40 to 80 feet (12 to 24 meters) high. These big waves can also break every 14 to 25 seconds. The first wave can pound a surfer deep under the water. The following waves can keep the surfer under for a very long time.

Big-wave surfers often need to be rescued. In the next chapter, you'll learn how such a rescue is done.

This towsurfer rides a big wave as the water patrol looks on.

A surfer shoots a curl on a big wave in Hawaii.

CHAPTER 3

Water Rescues

What does a water patrol team need to know?

How can team members keep a scared surfer calm?

How can the water patrol team stay calm?

What is the key to a safe rescue?

Facing the Risks

Surfers try to surf under the curl of a wave. They try to get inside the tube of air there. Yet, the falling curl can catch up to them. Tons of water can slam them deep under the water.

Water patrol team members can also get pushed underwater. Before they try to help, team members must think about the **risk** to themselves.

---

risk (RISK): danger

Much to Learn

Members of a water patrol team must know the ocean. They must learn how waves move. They must respect the ocean's power.

Team members must know themselves, too. They must know how long they can hold their breath. They need to know how strong they are.

Members must also know different ways to make a rescue. Sometimes, they have to dive into the water. Other times, they just need to throw a rescue ring or reach out a hand.

Sometimes, a rescue may not be possible. The waves might be too strong. A team is trained to make this hard **decision**.

---

decision (dee-SIZH-uhn): choice

A water patrol team looks for a surfer in pounding waves.

Stay Calm!

Brian Keaulana and Terry Ahue train rescue teams around the world. They teach the teams how to use a rescue sled. They help team members judge the risk in a rescue.

Mostly, Brian and Terry teach team members to stay calm. They coach them to control their fear. Panic can kill. If a rescue team is calm, a struggling surfer likely will stay calm, too. A scared surfer is hard to save. A scared rescue team is in big trouble!

Rescue teams must train for the worst. What training do you think they get? What kind of person would make a good team member? Would you?

This rescue team is heading out to help towsurfers off the shore.

Most rescue team members are lifeguards.
They know how to save lives. Still, they need
training to stay safe in big waves.

CHAPTER 4

Team Training

Imagine that you need to form a water rescue team.

What skills and knowledge will your team need?

What kind of people do you want on your team?

Getting Strong

A team is only as strong as its weakest **link**. On a water rescue team, the weakest link must be very strong.

To train, team members lift weights. Sometimes, they run **sprints** in soft sand. Other times, they run long distances. They often swim for 2 miles (3.2 kilometers). They may do 400 push-ups and sit-ups a day. Still, a strong body is not all that matters.

---

link (LINGK): a connection between things or people
sprint (SPRINT): a fast, short run

Getting Smart

Team members also train to drive the PWC. It's not easy to control a PWC in heavy **surf**. High waves can flip a PWC. Then the team might need to be rescued, too!

Teams learn safe ways to enter waves. Teams also learn when to stay out of waves. Team members practice keeping the PWC **steady**. That gives a team time to make a rescue.

Teams practice picking up and dropping off a surfer. They also learn how to pick up two surfers in one trip.

---

surf (SURF): the waves of the sea breaking on a shore or reef
steady (STED-ee): firm or stable; not shaky

Maui's Ocean Safety and Patrol holds classes to train rescue team members.

Staying Cool

Most rescue team members are lifeguards. They know how to save lives. Still, they must learn how to do this in big waves.

Teams must know how to carefully pick up a hurt surfer. They do not want to make an injury worse. They also learn how to rescue an **unconscious** surfer.

Teams must know how to find a surfer who has been pushed under the water. Team members must be able to hold their breath for a long, long time.

Could you hold your breath while waves beat down on you? Would you stay calm? Meet some rescue team members who can.

---

unconscious (uhn-KON-shuhss): not awake; not able to see, feel, or think

A surfer prepares to get hit really hard by tons of white water.

Brian Keaulana

CHAPTER 5

The Rescuers

Who do you think joins a water rescue team?

How do team members get started in this work?

What advice do rescue teams have for surfers?

Brian Keaulana

Brian Keaulana is a greatly respected surfer.
He first went surfing at just 3 months old.
His father took him out. His mother was not
happy about it!

Brian grew up to be a smart and safe surfer.
He formed the Hawaiian Water Patrol.
He also helped invent the rescue sled.

Today this sled saves lives around the world.
Brian tells surfers, "Surfing is the easy part.
Surviving is hard."

---

survive (sur-VIVE): to stay alive through a dangerous event

Archie Kalepa

Archie Kalepa (kuh-LEP-uh) has been surfing for more than 35 years. He helped Brian develop the rescue sled. Archie once used it in a **hurricane**. He saved 15 people and a dog.

Archie says, "Before you jump in, you better be sure there is an **exit**!" He teaches rescue teams to plan ahead. They must think about the risks. Then they will know whether to take the chance on a rescue.

Archie says it is safest to surf with friends. Surfers also must know their **limits**. They must know their friends' limits as well.

---

hurricane (HUR-uh-kane): a strong windstorm that forms over the ocean
exit (EG-zit): a way out
limit (LIM-it): the point where you can no longer safely do something

Archie Kalepa

Shawn Alladio

Not all rescue team members are men. Shawn Alladio (aw-LAH-dee-oh) started the K-38 Water Safety Program.

Shawn and her team teach rescue skills around the world. They even teach members of the U.S. Navy and Marines. The Coast Guard uses her program, too. Shawn says, "Know when to go." That means know when you should not go, too.

Shawn Alladio

Eric Akiskalian

You don't have to be a lifeguard to rescue big-wave surfers or help protect them. Eric Akiskalian (aw-kiss-KAY-lee-uhn) is a professional towsurfer. He formed the **Association** of **Professional** Towsurfers. This group puts on tow-in surfing events. It also gives surfers ocean safety information and training for big-wave surfing.

Eric Akiskalian

association (uh-soh-see-AY-shuhn): a club or group
professional (pruh-FESH-uh-nuhl): making money for something others do for fun

Darrick Doerner

Darrick Doerner (DOR-nur) has been surfing for more than 40 years. He helped start tow-in surfing. He is part of the Hawaiian Water Patrol. Darrick runs a camp for surfers, too.

Darrick says some people think tow-in surfing looks easy. It isn't, he reminds them. Yes, surfers get a ride out to the big waves. But surfing the big waves is another thing. Don't forget, says Darrick, a big wall of water is coming behind you! Surfers may wish they had not let go of the towrope!

Darrick tells surfers to know their limits. He tells them to try lots of small waves first. Then they might be ready for the big ones!

Darrick Doerner

How About You?

Would you like to big-wave surf? It takes years of learning and practice to train for these waves. Then it takes great **courage** to surf them. Is the **thrill** worth it to you?

courage (KUR-ij): bravery or fearlessness
thrill (THRIL): a strong feeling of excitement or pleasure

Epilogue

Eddie Would Go

Eddie Aikau (EYE-cow) is a surfing **legend**. Eddie was born on Maui (MOU-ee), Hawaii, in 1946. At age 13, he made his first surfboard. He had no money to buy one.

Eddie became a lifeguard. He saved hundreds of lives. When the waves got big, some lifeguards got scared. But Eddie would go to the rescue.

Eddie was one of the world's best surfers. Yet he was humble. He did not brag about his surfing. He did not talk about his rescues.

---

legend (LE-juhnd): someone whom people talk about and respect

Eddie Aikau

Eddie Did Go

Eddie was proud to be Hawaiian. In 1978, he and others began a special canoe trip. The group planned to paddle all the way to Tahiti (tah-HEE-tee). Long, long ago, Eddie's **ancestors** had made this same trip.

The first night, the canoe hit rough water. It turned over. The group hung on to it.

Eddie had brought along his surfboard. On it, he paddled for help. He tried to reach an island 12 miles (19 kilometers) away. No one ever saw Eddie again. The next night, the rest of the group was saved.

Now a big-wave surfing contest is named for Eddie. Surfers remember Eddie's bravery. They hope to be as brave as he was.

---

ancestor (AN-sess-tur): someone who comes earlier in a family line

This surfer is competing at the Quiksilver Eddie Aikau Big Wave Invitational contest.

Glossary

ancestor (AN-sess-tur): someone who comes earlier in a family line

association (uh-soh-see-AY-shuhn): a club or group

courage (KUR-ij): bravery or fearlessness

curl (KURL): the top of the wave as it bends over

decision (dee-SIZH-un): choice

exit (EG-zit): a way out

flee (FLEE): to run away

hurricane (HUR-uh-kane): a strong windstorm that forms over the ocean

legend (LE-juhnd): someone whom people talk about and respect

lifeguard (LIFE-gard): a person trained to save swimmers in danger

limit (LIM-it): the point where you can no longer safely do something

link (LINGK): a connection between things or people

panic (PAN-ik): to be affected by sudden, great fear

professional (pruh-FESH-uh-nuhl): making money for something others do for fun

risk (RISK): danger

slope (SLOHP): to slant or tilt

sprint (SPRINT): a fast, short run

steady (STED-ee): firm or stable; not shaky

surf (SURF): the waves of the sea breaking on a shore or reef

survive (sur-VIVE): to stay alive through a dangerous event

swell (SWEL): the top of a wave that has not fallen over

thrill (THRIL): a strong feeling of excitement or pleasure

tow (TOH): to pull something behind you

towboard (TOH-bord): a surfboard that has bindings on it to connect a surfer's feet to the board

towrope (TOH-rohp): a rope tied to a boat that pulls a surfer

unconscious (uhn-KON-shuhss): not awake; not able to see, feel, or think

Bibliography

Brimner, **Larry Dane**. *Surfing*. New York: Franklin Watts, 1997.

Crossingham, John and Bobbie Kalman. *Extreme Surfing*. Extreme Sports–No Limits! New York: Crabtree, 2004.

Mason, Paul. *Surfing*. To the Limit. A First Book. Austin, Texas: Raintree Steck-Vaughn, 2001.

Miller, Chuck. *Surfing*. Extreme Sports. Austin, Texas: Steadwell Books, 2002.

Useful Addresses

Association of Professional Towsurfers
6005 Northhill Loop S.W.
Olympia, WA 98512

Internet Sites

Association of Professional Towsurfers
http://www.protowsurfers.org

BeachLook
http://www.beachlook.com

Laird Hamilton
http://www.lairdhamilton.com

Shawn Alladio
http://www.shawnalladio.com

Towsurfer
http://www.towsurfer.com

Tow Surfing Adventures
http://www.towsurfingadventures.com

Index